BL: 6.6
Pts: 1.0

D0847830

Milton
Bradley

Other titles in the Inventors and Creators series include:

Alexander Graham Bell
Ben and Jerry
Roald Dahl
Walt Disney
Thomas Edison
Albert Einstein
Henry Ford
Benjamin Franklin
Jim Henson
Jonas Salk
Dr. Seuss
Steven Spielberg
The Wright Brothers

Milton
Bradley

Raymond H. Miller

KIDHAVEN PRESS
An imprint of Thomson Gale, a part of The Thomson Corporation

THOMSON
GALE

Detroit • New York • San Francisco • San Diego • New Haven, Conn. • Waterville, Maine • London • Munich

For more information, contact
KidHaven Press
27500 Drake Rd.
Farmington Hills, MI 48331-3535
Or you can visit our Internet site at http://www.gale.com

LIBRARY OF CONGRESS CATALOGING-IN-PUBLICATION DATA

Miller, Raymond H.
  Milton Bradley / by Raymond H. Miller.
    p. cm. — (Inventors and creators)
  Includes bibliographical references.
Summary: Discusses the life of Milton Bradley including his childhood, his training as a draftsman, the establishment of the Milton Bradley Company, and the games he and his company developed.
  ISBN 0-7377-2613-X (hardback : alk. paper)
  1. Milton Bradley Company. 2. Toy makers—Biography—Juvenile literature.
I. Title. II. Series.
  TS2301.T7M565 2004
  688.7'2'092—dc22

                                                  2004005454

Contents

Let the Games Begin

Like many great inventors of the nineteenth and twentieth centuries, Milton Bradley struggled to find success in the business world. He started out drawing pictures of other people's inventions. When the company he worked for went out of business, he decided to make a name for himself. He opened a new kind of printing press in Springfield, Massachusetts. It was the start of the Milton Bradley Company. The printing business was slow and Bradley was nearly out of money when he discovered a new interest—inventing games. Only then did he begin to realize his true talents. Combining his artistic ability with his technical knowledge, he designed a board game called The Checkered Game of Life. His timing could not have been better. The nation was engaged in the Civil War and people were looking for comfort. They found it in his new game. He soon created Games for Soldiers and Modern Hieroglyphics, which were also popular wartime games. The Milton Bradley Company went on to develop many more games and toys in the decades following the war. Eventually it became one of the most respected and successful game companies of the twentieth century. Some of its most well-known games include The Game of Life, Twister, and Candy Land.

Bradley did more than establish game playing as a regular part of American family life. He also had an impact on the field of education. He printed the first English-language manual promoting kindergarten. A firm believer that learning should be fun, Bradley later produced "Kindergarten Gifts," which included blocks, shapes, and small toys. The paint pigments he developed for the classroom made learning livelier and more enjoyable. Students could explore color by mixing the paints and brushing them onto paper. This hands-on technique reinforced what they were learning in class. By the early twentieth century, the Milton Bradley Company was the nation's leading provider of teaching aids, classroom furniture, and other school resources.

Bradley's work as a game inventor and educational pioneer has not been forgotten.

Milton Bradley dedicated his life to designing board games, teaching aids, and classroom furniture.

A group of friends plays Twister, a game the Milton Bradley Company first produced in the 1960s.

Nearly one hundred years after his death, modern games inspired by his creations continue to entertain and bring joy to people around the world.

Chapter One

A Young Man with a Plan

Milton Bradley was born in Vienna, Maine, on November 8, 1836. As the only child of Lewis and Fannie (Lyford) Bradley, Milton was the center of attention at home. He was an active child who needed almost constant attention from his mother. Lewis helped his wife tend to Milton whenever he could, but he worked long hours to provide for his family. He was a skilled craftsman who performed a variety of jobs at small, newly opened factories. But companies rarely stayed in business very long in those days, and Lewis was frequently laid off. When Milton was young, the Bradley family moved to many small towns in Maine and New Hampshire as Lewis went from job to job. No matter what job he found, he rarely earned a lot of money. His job at a cotton factory, for example, paid just thirty-five cents a day.

In the early 1840s it looked as though Lewis's fortunes might finally change for the better. While living in Mercer, Maine, he learned about the new process of

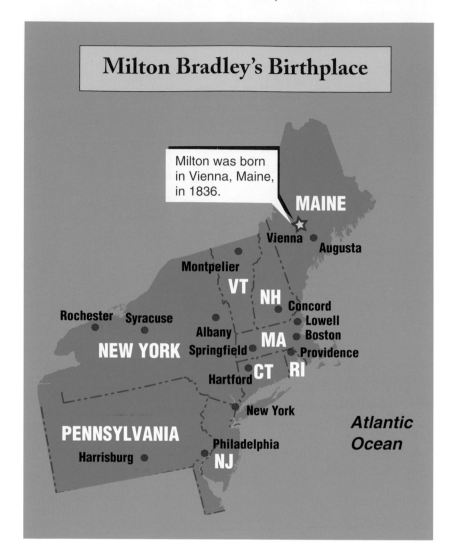

Milton Bradley's Birthplace

Milton was born in Vienna, Maine, in 1836.

MAINE

Vienna • Augusta

Montpelier

VT NH Concord

Rochester Syracuse • Lowell

Albany • Boston

NEW YORK Springfield • MA • Providence

Hartford CT RI

New York

PENNSYLVANIA Atlantic Ocean

Philadelphia

Harrisburg • NJ

making starch from potatoes. Starch was used as an ingredient in thickening food and making paper. For years he had been interested in going into business for himself. He researched the technique, purchased the necessary equipment, and opened Maine's first potato-starch factory. But in 1844 a potato rot disease struck Maine, wiping out crops throughout the state. Lewis had to close the factory and look for work elsewhere.

Lewis refused to become angry or disheartened because of his frequent layoffs and failed business. He and Fannie were very religious people. They accepted each setback in life as part of God's will, an outlook Milton also adopted. In 1846 the family moved to Mount Vernon, Maine. Within the year Lewis found a job in Lowell, Massachusetts, a rising industrial city near Boston. His family moved again.

Encouraged to Read

Many parents in the nineteenth century believed children should be seen and not heard. Lewis and Fannie saw things differently. They encouraged frequent conversation

When Milton was ten years old, the Bradley family moved to Lowell, an industrial city in Massachusetts.

with their son. They also took an active interest in his education. Reading became an important part of Milton's childhood. The family regularly took turns reading from the Bible as well as *Pilgrim's Progress, Poor Richard's Almanack,* and works of Shakespeare.

Playing Games

While Milton became an excellent reader by age six, he struggled in math. Adding and subtracting numbers simply did not make sense to him. Lewis decided to turn math into a game in hopes of helping his son. To demonstrate a basic subtraction problem, Lewis placed six red apples on the table and had Milton count them. Then he removed two apples and told his son to count them again. When Milton counted four apples and gave the correct answer, he was thrilled. With numbers representing *things,* math finally made sense to him. The young student excelled in math. His father's tabletop lesson did more than help Milton's grades, however. It taught him that learning was easier when it was fun.

Lewis and Fannie looked for other ways to give their son a joyful childhood. One was playing games together as a family. Their religious beliefs did not allow them to play cards. Card games were considered sinful because they involved chance. Checkers and chess were allowed because they required strategy and skill. Milton and his father spent many hours playing these games. Lewis encouraged his son to be a good sport when he lost, but Milton had a hard time hiding his excitement whenever he won.

An Interest in Art

Milton developed an interest in art while attending high school in Lowell. His drawings were realistic but simple, not overly stylish or showy. He later took an interest in watercolors and began painting.

After graduating from high school in 1854, Milton found a job that allowed him to make use of his artistic skills. He went to work as a **mechanical draftsman** for Oliver E. Cushman, a local draftsman and **patent agent**. He sketched the designs of machines invented by local citizens who had hopes of getting a U.S. patent. The work gave Milton the idea that he, too, might join the pioneer spirit sweeping New England. He thought about opening his own patent office. But his goal at the time was simply to earn enough money to afford the three-hundred-dollar admission to Lawrence Scientific School at nearby Harvard. Milton sold stationery supplies in his spare time to add to the income he made at the

As a young man, Milton worked for a patent office, sketching machine designs.

patent office. Although he was fresh out of high school, he showed good business sense. He knew the best time to sell his goods was when potential customers had plenty of money. He later explained:

> As a certain portion of the corporations paid off each week, I always selected the days when the girls were "flush" [just received cash]. . . . I, in fact, had an *established* trade which competitors who learned my methods tried in vain to take from me, as the girls would wait for me.[1]

Before long Milton had saved the money necessary to enroll in a two-year drafting program at the Lawrence Scientific School. He lived at home and commuted to school daily. In the middle of his second year at school, however, his plans changed abruptly. His parents moved to Hartford, Connecticut, so Lewis could take a job there. This left Milton without a place to stay. He reluctantly left school and moved to Hartford. He was disappointed that his education was cut short, although he never blamed his father. He had learned long ago from Lewis that the best way to deal with disappointment was to accept it and move on.

Looking for an Opportunity

Milton immediately began looking for a drafting position in Hartford. With jobs in short supply, he turned his attention to Springfield, Massachusetts. He had heard Springfield was one of the great industrial centers in New England. Anyone who wanted an opportunity and was willing to work hard would find it there. He packed a single suitcase and boarded a train for Springfield. As the train approached the city, Milton was amazed by what he saw. Thick black smoke poured out of the foundries and factories, filling the sky like a dark cloud. When he stepped off the train, he was greeted with the loud clatter of Springfield's booming industries. All that he had heard seemed to be true. The city *was* taking part in something important, the industrialization of America. He quickly set out to become a part of it.

In 1856 Milton moved to Springfield, Massachusetts, in search of work as a draftsman.

Milton was confident that he could do well in Springfield as a draftsman. Even so, he was nervous as he walked into the Wason Car-Manufacturing Company on his first day in Springfield to ask for a job. The company designed and manufactured railroad cars, something Milton found fascinating but knew little about. He told the company superintendent that he had a steady drawing hand and a good eye for proportion and balance. He added that he was knowledgeable in mechanics. When the superintendent asked Milton if he could draw a train car, the young man replied confidently, "I never have, but I think I could."[2] The superintendent doubted that someone so young and inexperienced could do the job. However, he saw something in Milton that he liked and hired him on the spot. The teenager was thrilled.

Work in the drafting department at the Wason Company was not fancy or glamorous. The starting pay was less than ten dollars a week, and the workplace was dark, smoky, and cramped. Milton kept a positive attitude. Not yet twenty years old, he had a job in a bustling city filled with creative people. He was eager to contribute his talents and ideas.

Chapter Two

The Milton Bradley Company

Milton started his job in the drafting department at the Wason Company in the summer of 1856. Working for an established company at the center of a thriving industrial city was a thrill for this young man several months shy of his twentieth birthday. Living away from home for the first time only added to his excitement.

Milton loved his job at the Wason Company. He found something romantic about the railroad industry. Still, he began making plans for opening his own drafting company and patent office. To reach his goal he knew he needed money and experience, and the only way to get either was by working at the Wason Company. Over the next six months Milton became a skilled draftsman and learned how locomotives and train cars worked.

By the beginning of 1857, New England was suffering from a **recession**. Businesses were failing because of the economic slowdown. Fortunately for

At the age of nineteen, Milton Bradley began working as a draftsman for the Wason Company (pictured).

Milton there was still a demand for locomotives and train cars, and the Wason Company stayed in business. By the summer of 1858, however, the growing division between northern and southern states over slavery and other issues caused a financial panic that wiped out five thousand businesses nationwide. The Wason Company, with no orders for locomotive and train cars, was forced to close. Milton was out of work, wondering what to do next.

Saved by the Viceroy

Despite the bad economy, Milton believed it was time to open his own drafting company and patent office. Inventors would still need mechanical drawings and patents for their contraptions, he reasoned. On a September morning in 1858 he hung a sign on the door of a small, second-floor office on Main Street in Springfield. He was open for business.

Around this time, Milton started dating a woman named Vilona Eaton. The two met through a mutual friend and fell in love. With the future in question, Milton was unsure about asking her to marry him. As it turned out he had made the right decision. The recession had left inventors with few funds to pay Milton, and he was losing money fast.

Through fall and early winter, business was still slow and Milton was preparing to close his office. Then the Wason Company contacted him. The company had just received a $300,000 order for custom train cars from Isma'il Pasha, the **viceroy** of Egypt. Factory officials wanted to hire Milton back to work on the massive project. Eager to make money so he could buy an engagement ring for Vilona, Milton agreed. He immediately started working

Milton designed a custom train car for Isma'il Pasha, the viceroy of Egypt (pictured).

on a mechanical drawing for Pasha's personal train car. Wason Company officials were so impressed by his drawing that they asked him to supervise the construction of the car. Milton accepted and spent the next several months overseeing production. He earned enough money to finally buy an engagement ring for Vilona. The two would marry on November 8, 1860—his twenty-fourth birthday.

Start the Press

When Pasha's elaborate train car was finished, the Wason Company ordered a color **lithograph** print of the car. They presented it to Milton in appreciation of the fine work he had done. He was proud of the car but seemed more impressed with the picture. He hung it on the wall and stared at it for hours. **Lithography** was a relatively new printing process in the United

The Wason Company gave Milton this lithograph of the train car he designed for Pasha.

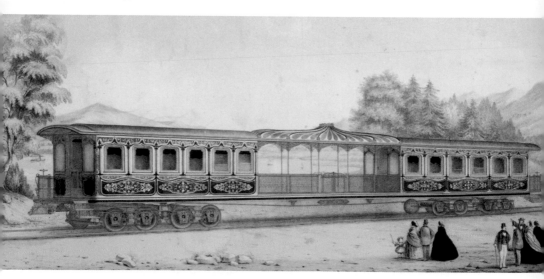

States, and there were no such printing presses in Springfield. Before long, Milton could think of nothing but opening his own lithograph business. He went to visit a childhood friend named George Tapley, who worked at a Providence, Rhode Island, printing press that did lithograph work. Milton stayed with Tapley, who arranged for his friend to become an **apprentice** under the master press operator.

By January 1860, Milton's training at the printing press was complete. He bought a lithograph press in Providence and had it delivered to Springfield. He set it up in the drafting room of the Wason Company. "And here my troubles began," he said later. "In fact, my first real troubles came with the lithograph business."[3] That did not appear to be the case at first, however. The printing orders came pouring in. By May he was having trouble keeping up with orders and had outgrown his office space. He moved to a building down the street and set up his press in a much larger room. He tossed aside his old sign and made a new one. In bold letters it read:

Milton Bradley Company
Publishers
Lithographers

Honest Abe

Several months after starting his printing press, Milton found himself involved in politics. The year 1860 was a presidential election year. The Republican Party asked

Milton to do a very special job. They wanted him to produce a lithograph of their candidate for president, Abraham Lincoln. Like most New Englanders, Milton strongly opposed slavery and he admired Lincoln for taking a stand against it. The young lithographer gladly accepted the job and began making prints of a young, clean-shaven

In 1860 Milton set up his own lithography and publishing business in Springfield.

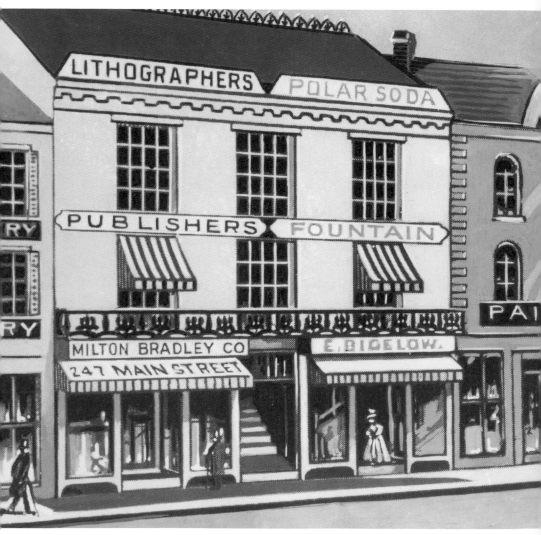

Lincoln. Things did not go smoothly, however. He experienced frequent delays due to mechanical problems with the press. He also had trouble finding a capable press operator. Milton ran many of the prints himself. He made up for the lost time by working around the clock. Finally his office was stacked high with prints of the future president.

The Lincoln lithographs sold extremely well throughout New England in the months before the election. Even after Lincoln won the election and took office, sales were steady. It appeared Milton had finally found

Milton created this lithograph of Abraham Lincoln for the 1860 presidential election.

success in the business world. Then one day a man who had bought a Lincoln lithograph barged into Milton's office and complained that the print looked nothing like the new president. Lincoln had grown a beard after taking office, the man told him. The prints were no longer any good. Few people wanted an outdated picture of the president, and sales of the prints came to a halt. Some customers even demanded their money back.

Milton could not believe the sudden turn of events. He threw the lithographs away, losing thousands of potential dollars. Like his father, Milton did not let this failure keep him down for long. He was about to embark on a new and exciting business venture.

Chapter Three

The Checkered Game of Life

In the summer of 1860, just before Bradley received the order for the Lincoln lithograph, longtime friend George Tapley paid him a visit. Tapley brought along an old English game that was played on a board with oval disks. Bradley was fascinated with the game, and the two men played for hours. When Tapley left, his friend felt uplifted and that night an idea came to his mind. He was going to develop his own game that he could lithograph, package, and sell through the Milton Bradley Company.

For several weeks Bradley worked on his new game. He designed a board with sixty-four alternating white and red squares. The white squares were labeled with either good or bad values, such as "truth" and "honor" or "disgrace" and "crime." The red squares were neutral. He also devised a spinner so players would know how many squares they were to move their game pieces. The object was to reach "Happy Old Age" while trying to avoid "Ruin." He called it The Checkered Game of Life.

Bradley finished a sample of his game and took it to Tapley so the two could play. Tapley was impressed. He had good business instincts and became convinced the game would sell. Bradley trusted his friend's judgment and quickly went to work printing several hundred game boards on his press. An assistant cut and packaged the game boards. Bradley placed the games in a large case and set off for New York City by train. During the trip he nervously wondered if the public would enjoy his game as much as he and Tapley had.

In 1860 Bradley invented The Checkered Game of Life, a board game that was educational and fun.

Games for Soldiers

On a cold fall afternoon in 1861, Bradley was walking to his job at the armory. He spotted some Union soldiers warming themselves around a campfire. He could tell by their somber faces that they needed a morale boost. Although he had put The Checkered Game of Life on hold because of the war, he had decided to spend his free time making a smaller version of the game. This one would be just for soldiers. He included it as part of a collection with eight other miniature games: chess, checkers, backgammon, and five varieties

Union soldiers play a game of dominoes in this 1863 photo.

of dominoes. This was the first time someone assembled multiple games in one package. Calling it Games for Soldiers, Bradley gave game kits to soldiers around Springfield. He was pleased when he saw them playing the games and laughing. It occurred to him that people across the war-weary nation might enjoy playing them, too. Bradley sent a description of the kit to the store owners who had bought his first game. Then he waited to see if the idea would catch on.

In just a few months Bradley knew he had found his next big seller. Store owners placed thousands of orders for the game kits, putting the Milton Bradley Company back in business for good. While the war raged on, Bradley and his helpers worked overtime to keep up with orders. Just as Bradley had hoped, families played the nine little games as a way to take their minds off the war. And they were not the only ones buying Games for Soldiers. Charitable organizations purchased huge quantities of the game kits and gave them to Union army soldiers across the battlefield.

Losing Vilona

Bradley spent the next few years developing more games, including a new version of the ancient puzzle known as a rebus. He called it Modern Hieroglyphics, or Picture Writings for the Times. The object of the game was to build sentences using picture and word cards. Bradley wanted the game to be educational as well as fun, so he made the pictures and words related to modern subjects, such as the Civil War. People were

Bradley's Myrioptican brought to life Civil War scenes like this one.

so enthusiastic about the game that they began sending their own rebuses to Bradley. If he liked an idea and used it in a later edition, he sent money in return.

In 1864 the company expanded and Bradley hired two men, one of them George Tapley's brother, to oversee operations. This arrangement allowed Bradley to concentrate entirely on game and toy development. He soon created a toy called The Myrioptican, a round device that contained a series of lithograph prints. When a person turned a crank, the moving pictures formed a Civil War scene that appeared to be in motion. The toy caught on just as the war was ending and it continued to amaze audiences for many years to come. Other Bradley achievements during the decade were the fifteen-square slide puzzle, the first mass-produced croquet set, and a Parcheesi-like game called Ludo that was sold overseas.

Bradley's company mass-produced croquet sets like the one enjoyed by this family.

At age thirty Bradley was enjoying success as a game inventor when Vilona became ill. Her health declined over the winter, and she died on March 13, 1867. For weeks Bradley grieved. He had no interest in fun and games. It seemed that all the work he had done to turn a small printing company into the nation's leading game manufacturer had been for nothing.

Chapter Four

Kindergarten Pioneer

The weeks following Vilona's death were extremely difficult for Bradley. Only after his parents moved in with him did he go back to work creating or improving games and toys. The Zoetrope, or Wheel of Life, was an improved version of The Myrioptican. Patented by Bradley in 1867, The Zoetrope was an open-top drum with thirteen slits and a series of fourteen figures inside, all shown in phases of motion. When a person spun The Zoetrope and looked through the slits, the figures appeared to be in motion. The toy was an instant success and remained a popular item for forty years.

Bradley did not spend all his time developing games. In late 1868 he met a woman named Ellen "Nellie" Thayer. The two had a brief engagement and married the next spring. They later had two daughters, Florence and Lillian. Around the time Bradley met Nellie, his career took another turn. He became excited after attending a speech given by Elizabeth

Peabody. She had established the nation's first kindergarten and was trying to generate interest in starting one in Springfield. Bradley put game and toy development on hold to publish a book called *Paradise of Childhood, a Practical Guide to Kindergartners*. It was the first illustrated guide to kindergarten printed in the English language. Bradley later started a kindergarten in Springfield. He, along with his father and Nellie, taught the school's first two students—Florence and Lillian.

When seen through the slits in the spinning drum of the Zoetrope, the figures on the strip seem to move.

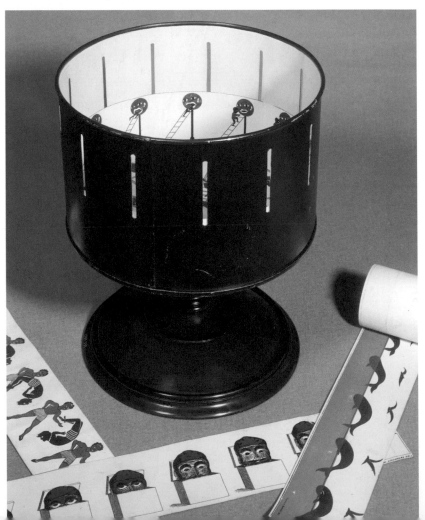

Bradley spent more and more time developing kindergarten products. He eventually decided to expand his company to include an educational division. Bradley's decision did not please his business partners. They were convinced the new division would take money away from the company's line of games. Sales were already down because the U.S. economy was suffering from a postwar **depression**. Unemployment was high, businesses were closing, and people were spending less money, especially on items such as games and toys. But Bradley was persistent. He believed that if the company produced quality educational products and offered them at affordable prices, they would sell well.

Learning Is Fun

Bradley kept recalling how his father had taught him to add and subtract with apples. He thought teaching tools made learning fun, and he was eager to share this belief with educators. One man who shared Bradley's philosophy was his friend, George Tapley. In 1878 Tapley bought out Bradley's partners and started managing operations at the company. In the meantime Bradley developed blocks, toys, and other small playthings for teaching basic learning skills in a fun way. He called them "Kindergarten Gifts." In time "Kindergarten Gifts" became a regular part of nursery schools and kindergartens throughout the United States.

Bradley's work in education did not stop there. He also developed a new way to teach children about color. For months he worked with local art teachers on creating easy-to-use paint **pigments**. After finally developing a satisfactory product, he sent the pigments to schools in powder form. By simply adding water, teachers and students could have bright, even colors. Bradley's pigments set the standard for teaching about color in the classroom. He later wrote and published four books on the subject, including *Elementary Color*. Bradley's innovation had already gained the respect and trust of teachers when his company began producing classroom furniture. By the late nineteenth century the Milton Bradley Company was providing schools with a wide range of supplies and equipment, from chairs and desks to paper cutters and easels.

Years later, when kindergarten had become an established part of the U.S. public school system, Bradley wrote an article in the *Kindergarten Review*. In the article he summed up his feelings about the contributions he had made to kindergarten:

> In using the word success, I do not wish to confine its meaning to that cheap interpretation which sees only the glitter of gold or the glamour of illusive fame. In my case, I cannot overestimate the feeling of satisfaction which has been with me all these years at the thought that I have been identified with this movement and have done something, if only something [ordinary] in character, to place the kindergarten on its present solid foundation.[5]

Bradley's company developed equipment and supplies for kindergarten classrooms like this one.

Down

be an important part of
ny well into the twentieth
sure his company remained
velopment. In 1880 he cre-
ocomotive—the first jigsaw
ars later, when Buffalo Bill's
ular with kids, the company
ll Gun, a toy gun that shot
wooden pellets. It was the company's most popular toy
yet. Bradley also developed a lawn game called En-
chantment. Players used wands to try to toss hoops
into a designated area without opposing players catch-
ing or knocking the hoops away.

At the turn of the century, the Milton Bradley
Company was a highly successful business selling hun-
dreds of games, toys, and educational tools. The company that had started inside a cramped office forty
years earlier now occupied several large buildings in
Springfield. Bradley's company was one of the largest
in the world, and he could not have been prouder.

Bradley remained active in the company well into
his sixties. When his health began to decline, Tapley
and others took over making all the business decisions.
In 1907, at the age of seventy, Bradley retired from the
work he loved.

The Games Go On

On May 27, 1911, Milton and Nellie drove through
Springfield. They waved to old friends they passed and

smiled at children playing croquet on front lawns. The next day, Milton suddenly became ill and never recovered. Two days later, with his wife at his bedside, he quietly passed away. He was seventy-four years old. Springfield mourned the loss of one of its brightest and most beloved citizens. At the Milton Bradley Company, saddened workers stopped in honor of his passing, while company officials issued a statement

In 1880 Bradley created The Smashed Up Locomotive, the first jigsaw puzzle designed for children.

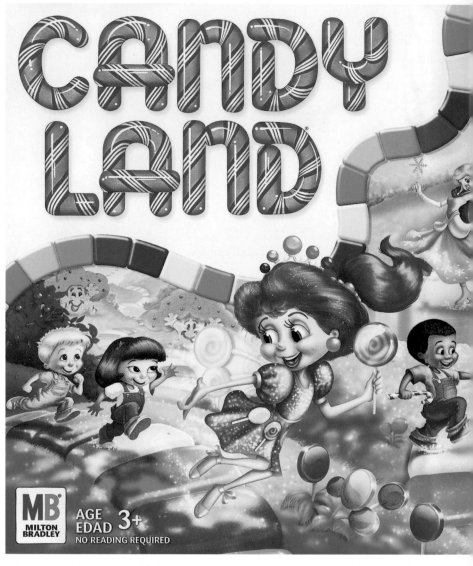

that read in part, "Though the man is called, his work lives after him, a lasting memorial to his ingenuity, nobleness of purpose and strength of character."[6]

After Bradley's death his company grew and prospered as it continued to sell successful games in the mid-1900s. These included Chutes and Ladders, Candy Land, and Twister.

Candy Land is one of many games the Milton Bradley Company has developed since Bradley's death.

The Milton Bradley Company remained committed to its founder's love for educational products. It bought Playskool, Inc., a leader in early childhood toys and learning tools. But in 1984, Hasbro, another popular game company, purchased the Milton Bradley Company along with Playskool, Inc. Even so, Hasbro continues to package the games under the Milton Bradley name, securing a place in history for one of the world's most popular and respected game and toy inventors.

Notes

Chapter One: A Young Man with a Plan

1. Milton Bradley Company, *Milton Bradley: A Successful Man.* Springfield, MA: Milton Bradley, 1910, p. 5.
2. Quoted in James J. Shea and Charles Mercer, *It's All in the Game.* New York: Putnam, 1960, p. 20.

Chapter Two: The Milton Bradley Company

3. Quoted in Shea and Mercer, *It's All in the Game,* p. 42.

Chapter Three: The Checkered Game of Life

4. G. Wayne Miller, *Toy Wars: The Epic Struggle Between G.I. Joe, Barbie, and the Companies That Make Them.* New York: Times Books, 1998, p. 40.

Chapter Four: Kindergarten Pioneer

5. Quoted in Shea and Mercer, *It's All in the Game,* p. 180.
6. Quoted in Shea and Mercer, *It's All in the Game,* p. 183.

Glossary

apprentice: A person who works under an experienced professional to learn an art, craft, or trade.

depression: A period of time in which the economy is in steep decline, resulting in high unemployment, low output, and poverty.

lithograph: A print made by lithography.

lithography: A printing process in which the image to be printed receives the ink and the blank area repels the ink.

mechanical draftsman: A person who makes mechanical, or highly technical, drawings of objects that work or move.

patent agent: A person who attempts to secure a patent for an invention, charging the inventor a fee for doing so.

pigment: A substance that adds black or white or a color to another material.

recession: A moderate and sometimes extended slowdown in business activity.

viceroy: The governor of a country, province, or colony who rules as the representative of a king.

For Further Exploration

Books

R.C. Bell, *Board and Table Games from Many Civilizations*. Mineola, NY: Dover, 1980. Provides useful information about the history of games from around the world.

Bobbie Kalman and David Schimpky, *Old-Time Toys*. New York: Crabtree, 1995. A fascinating look back at nineteenth-century playthings.

James J. Shea and Charles Mercer, *It's All in the Game*. New York: Putnam, 1960. A detailed account of Milton Bradley's life and how he became the greatest game inventor of his time.

Don Wulffson, *Toys! Amazing Stories Behind Some Great Inventions*. New York: Henry Holt, 2000. A collection of interesting stories behind the creation of LEGO bricks, Mr. Potato Head, Twister, and more.

Web Sites

Hasbro (www.hasbro.com). The official Web site of Hasbro provides a brief look at the history of the Milton Bradley Company and lists a number of Milton Bradley "firsts."

Milton Bradley (www.quadrangle.org). Contains a brief profile of Milton Bradley's start in the game business and includes his accomplishments.

Index

Picture Credits

About the Author

Raymond H. Miller is the author of more than fifty nonfiction books for children. He has written on a range of topics from poisonous animals to presidential trivia. He enjoys playing sports and spending time outdoors with his wife and two daughters.